SEEMANNSMISSION
Traum aller Nixen – Alain Delon in
»Nur die Sonne war Zeuge«, 1960.

SEAMEN'S MISSION
The dream of all mermaids – Alain
Delon in »Plein Soleil«, 1960.

BEHNKEN & PRINZ

STARS ON BOARD

DIE SCHÖNSTE BÜHNE DER WELT UND IHRE HAUPTDARSTELLER
THE WORLD'S MOST BEAUTIFUL STAGE AND THEIR LEADING ACTORS

DELIUS KLASING VERLAG

THRONSAAL
Ein Ständchen für die Königin: Elisabeth II. und Prinz Philip besuchen 1977 mit der »HMY Britannia« die Fidschi-Inseln.

THRONE ROOM
A serenade for the Queen: Elizabeth II and Prince Philip on a trip to the Fiji Islands aboard the »HMY Britannia« in 1977.

SEITE / PAGE 16
GEKRÖNTE HÄUPTER
CROWNED HEADS

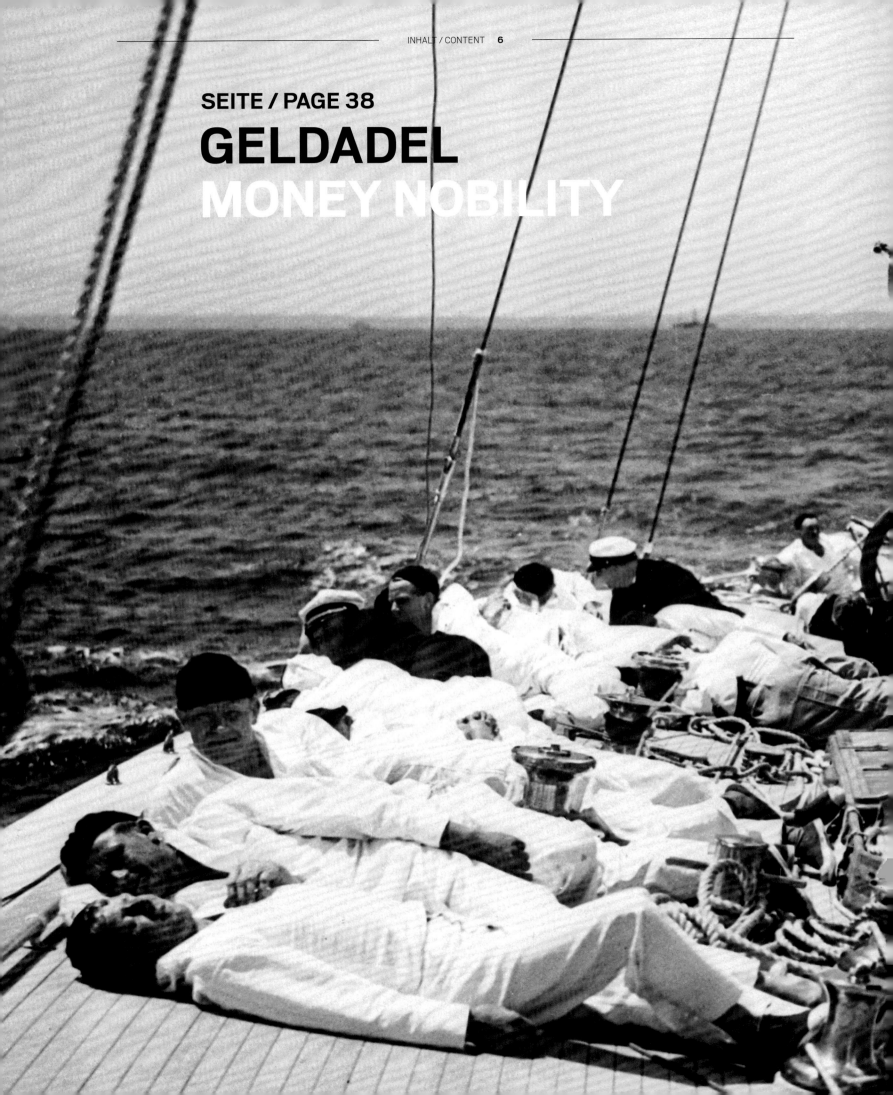

INHALT / CONTENT 6

SEITE / PAGE 38
GELDADEL
MONEY NOBILITY

SPORTPLATZ
Harold S. Vanderbilt und Crew kämpfen 1937 vor Rhode Island im America's Cup um die Krone des Segelns.

SPORTS FIELD
Harold S. Vanderbilt and his crew at the America's Cup battling for the crown of sailing off the coast of Rhode Island in 1937.

SPIELPLATZ
Rapper P. Diddy wirft seinen weiblichen Fans im Yachthafen von St. Tropez Autogrammkarten zu.

PLAYGROUND
Rapper P. Diddy tossing autograph cards towards his female fans in the marina of St. Tropez.

POLITISCHE BÜHNE
John F. Kennedy und seine Verlobte Jacqueline beim Segelausflug 1953. Das Foto ist Teil einer ausgefeilten PR-Strategie.

POLITICAL STAGE
John F. Kennedy and his fiancée Jacqueline on a sailing trip in 1953. This photograph is part of an elaborate PR strategy.

SEITE / PAGE 90
KLUGE KÖPFE
SMART MINDS

INHALT / CONTENT **12**

SEITE / PAGE 118
FILM AB
SHOWTIME

TANZTHEATER
Auf einem Schiff im Ärmelkanal trotzt ein Piratensender der britischen Regierung – eine Szene aus »Radio Rock Revolution«.

DANCE THEATRE
A pirate radio station aboard a ship in the Channel defies the British government – a scene from »Radio Rock Revolution«.

INGRID BERGMAN mit ihren vier Kindern bei einem Bootsauflug 1957 in Italien.
INGRID BERGMAN with her four children during a boat trip in Italy in 1957.

W

Was verbindet Königin Elizabeth II. mit Wladimir Putin? Was eint Grace Kelly mit John F. Kennedy und Albert Einstein? Was haben Brigitte Bardot und Andy Warhol, Errol Flynn und Lady Di gemein?
Sie sind Meister im Fach der Selbstdarstellung. Boote sind ihre Bühne. Ihre Kulisse ist die See. Und ihr Publikum sitzt an Land und klatscht für weitere Zugaben.
Kaum gehen Stars an Bord, machen sie eine auffällige Wandlung durch. So wird aus einem eher introvertierten Physiker ein Herzensbrecher. Ein kühler Rechner wird unter dem Einfluss seiner Megayacht zu einem kühnen Eroberer. Ein gewiefter Staatsmann lebt endlich seinen geheimen Spieltrieb aus. Ein berüchtigter Mafiaboss entdeckt seine Leidenschaft für kleine Fische. Ein Modedesigner glaubt auf einmal, dass er über's Wasser gehen kann. Eine brave Prinzessin lässt Drachen rudern. Eine Schauspielerin legt einen begehrten Junggesellen an die Ankerkette.
Was aber ist der Grund dafür, dass sich Stars an Bord so sehr verändern? Ist es vielleicht die salzhaltige Seeluft, ist es der schwankende Boden oder die Sonne, die ihr Verhalten beeinflusst? Ist es vielleicht sogar die Sehnsucht nach dem Meer, nach grenzenloser Freiheit und unendlichen Weiten,

H

How are Queen Elizabeth II and Vladimir Putin connected? What unites Grace Kelly, John F. Kennedy and Albert Einstein? What do Brigitte Bardot and Andy Warhol, Errol Flynn and Lady Di have in common?
They are masters of self-promotion. Boats are their stages. The sea is their backdrop. Their audience sits ashore and claps for more and more encores.
As soon as stars go aboard, they undergo a conspicuous transition. Thus a rather introverted physicist becomes a heartbreaker. Under the influence of his mega yacht a cool reckoner becomes a bold conqueror. A smart statesman finally acts out his secret play instinct. A notorious mafia boss discovers his passion for small fish. A fashion designer all of a sudden believes that he can walk on the water. A well-behaved princess makes dragons row. An actress puts a sought-after bachelor on the anchor chain.
However, what is the reason why the stars change so much on board? Is it the salty sea air, does the swaying ground or the sun affect their behaviour? Maybe it is even the longing for the sea, for an unlimited freedom and the boundless vastness which slumbers in every human being and which finally forges? Or is this part of an elaborate PR strategy like

GRACE KELLY in Cannes 1955 – ein Jahr vor ihrer Märchenhochzeit mit Fürst Rainier.
GRACE KELLY IN CANNES 1955 – one year before her dream wedding with Prince Rainier.

die in jedem Menschen schlummert und sich endlich Bahn bricht? Oder ist das alles vielleicht Teil einer ausgefeilten PR-Strategie, wie sie einst für John F. Kennedy entwickelt wurde und hunderte Male kopiert worden ist?
Um der Öffentlichkeit das Bild eines sportlichen, vitalen, freiheitsliebenden und lebenshungrigen Präsidenten zu vermitteln, setzte sich Kennedy wie kein anderer Politiker auf Booten in Szene. Zugleich spielte er den Wählern die Rolle des treusorgenden Vaters vor, lenkte von Affären und einem Rückenleiden ab, das ihn zwang, immer ein Korsett zu tragen.
Wladimir Putin wandelt heute auf Kennedys Spuren. Fotos von ihm auf einem Boot haben immer etwas Martialisches an sich: Putin im U-Boot, Putin in Tarnkleidung am Steuer eines Motorboots – jedes Bild für sich trägt die gleiche Botschaft: »Ich bin ein ganzer Kerl.«
Meister dieser Wasserspiele waren auch Grace Kelly und Fürst Rainier von Monaco. Sie haben den Hafen von Monte Carlo zu einer riesigen Freilichtbühne gemacht. Dort inszenierten sie ihre Ehe zum Wohle des Steuerparadieses. Und dort gaben in ihrem Fahrwasser viele internationale Stars in Komödien und Tragödien gefeierte Gastspiele.
Von Menschen wie diesen erzählt dieses Buch.

it was developed for John F. Kennedy and copied hundreds of times?
In order to present the public an image of a sporty, energetic, freedom-loving and zestful president, Kennedy used to put himself in the limelight on boats as no other politician. At the same time feigned the role of the devoted father to his voters, he diverted attention from his love affairs and his back problems forcing him to always wear a corset.
Today, Vladimir Putin is walking in Kennedy's footsteps. Photos of him on a boat always look slightly martial: Putin in a submarine, Putin in camouflage at the helm of a motorboat – each photo has the same message: »I am a real man.«
Also Grace Kelly and Prince Rainier of Monaco were masters of these water games. They transformed the harbour of Monte Carlo into a huge open air stage. There they staged their marriage for the good of the tax haven. In their channel many international stars gave guest performances in comedies and tragedies.
This book tells about people like these.

GEKRÖNTE HÄUPTER
CROWNED HEADS

Lange Zeit war die Seefahrt Abenteurern, Entdeckern, Freibeutern, Handels- und Kriegsmarine vorbehalten. Erst im 18. Jahrhundert entdeckten Kaiser und Könige vermehrt Yachten als Bühne der Eitelkeiten ...

Seafaring has long been reserved for adventurers, explorers, buccaneers, merchants and the navy. Only in the 18th century emperors and kings more and more discovered the yachts as a stage for vanities...

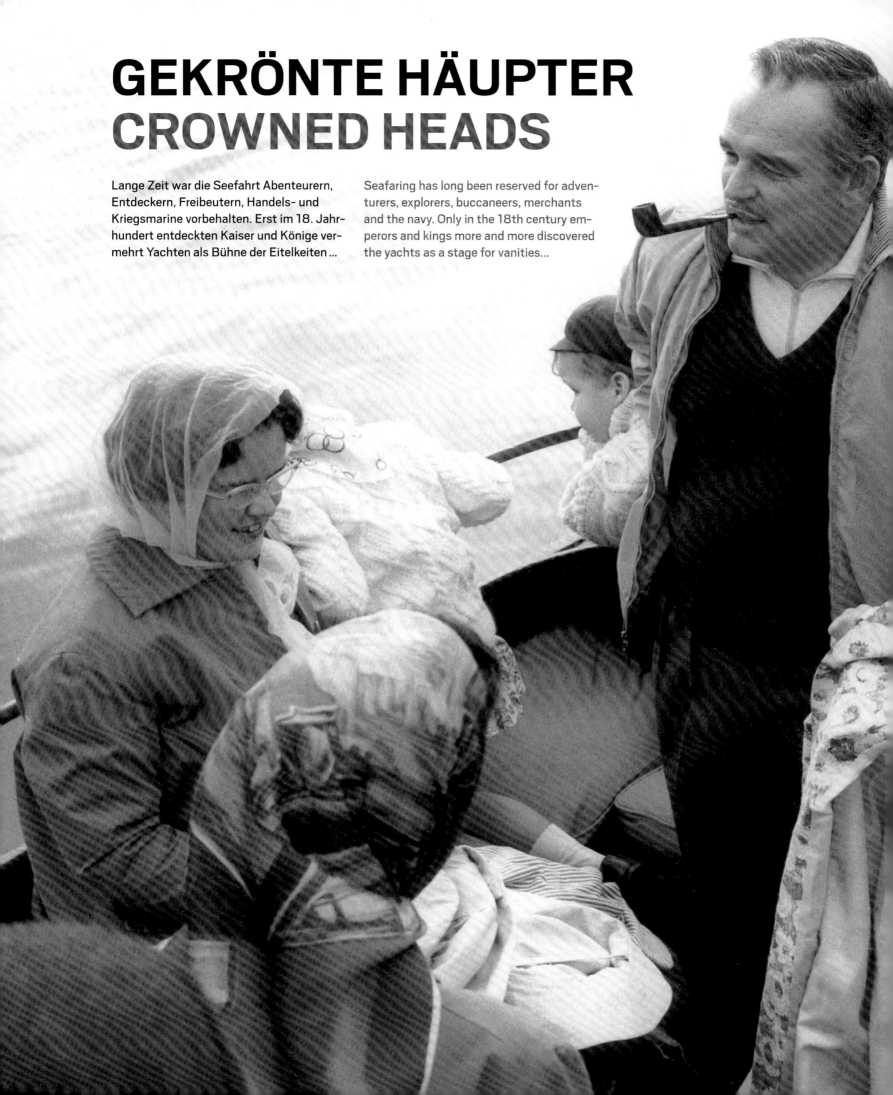

GASTSPIEL
Die monegassische Fürstenfamilie hat ihre Bühne Monte Carlo verlassen und besucht 1961 Irland. Während sich Rainier III. weltmännisch gibt, begutachtet Fürstin Grace Stoffe von Näherinnen aus der Region.

AWAY GAME
The Monegasque Princely Family has left their stage of Monte Carlo and visits Ireland in 1961. While Rainier III. is acting suavely, Princess Grace examines materials produced by seamstresses from the region.

GEKRÖNTE HÄUPTER / CROWNED HEADS **18**

RUDERGÄNGER Prinz Albert, 1975.
HELMSMAN Prince Albert, 1975.

LAUFSTEG ▶
Grace Kelly wurde auf der Schiffsreise von New York nach Monaco auf Schritt und Tritt von ihrem Hund und 100 Reportern begleitet.

CATWALK
On the sea trip from New York to Monaco Grace Kelly was accompanied at every turn by her dog and 100 reporters.

Man stelle sich das einmal vor: Der beinahe bankrotte Fürst eines Zwergenstaates, nur halb so groß wie der Centralpark in New York, heiratet einen Filmstar – und rettet damit die Dynastie vor dem Untergang. Überdies ist die Braut Oscar-Preisträgerin, gilt als beste Partie Hollywoods und ist die Tochter eines amerikanischen Millionärs. Was sich wie ein schmalziges Drehbuch liest, hat sich tatsächlich so zugetragen. Die Liebesgeschichte zwischen Rainier III. von Monaco und Grace Kelly (»Die oberen Zehntausend«) war die Sensation des Jahres 1956. Die Trauung war von den MGM-Studios wie ein Spielfilm geplant und inszeniert worden: 2000 Reporter und Fotografen waren aus aller Welt angereist, Hunderte davon gemeinsam mit der Braut auf dem Kreuzfahrtschiff »Constitution«. Unter den illustren Partygästen waren König Faruq von Ägypten, der Aga Khan, Aristoteles Onassis, Cary Grant und Ava Gardner – und 30 Millionen Fernsehzuschauer weltweit verfolgten live, wie sich das Paar das Ja-Wort gab. Wie die Hochzeit, so führten die Grimaldis auch ihre Ehe – auf der Bühne Monaco. Eine vergleichbare Familieninszenierung hat es seither nie wieder gegeben.

Just imagine: The nearly bankrupt prince of a mini-state, only half as large as the Central Park in New York, marries a movie star – and hence saves the dynasty from extinction. Moreover, the bride is an Oscar-winning actress, she is considered the best catch in Hollywood and the daughter of an American millionaire. What one could read as a sentimental script has actually happened that way. The love story between Rainier III. of Monaco and Grace Kelly (»High Society«) was the sensation of the year 1956. The wedding ceremony was planned and directed like a feature film by the MGM Studios: 2000 reporters and photographers had come from all over the world, hundreds of them together with the bride on board the cruise ship »Constitution«. Among the illustrious party guests there were King Farouq of Egypt, the Aga Khan, Aristoteles Onassis, Cary Grant and Ava Gardner – and 30 million television viewers around the world watched live as the couple made their vows. The Grimaldi family lived their marriage just like their wedding – on the stage of Monaco. A similar family staging has never since been seen.

GEKRÖNTE HÄUPTER / CROWNED HEADS 21

BOOTSMANN Juan Carlos, 1959 mit einem Freund in St. Tropez (oben, links) und 1990 mit Prinz Charles, Lady Di und Familie an Bord seiner Yacht »Fortuna«.

BOATSWAIN Juan Carlos in 1959 with a friend in St. Tropez (top left) and in 1990 with Prince Charles, Lady Di and family on board his yacht »Fortuna«.

◀ **KÖNIGSKLASSE**
Juan Carlos, der Olympionike: 1972 nahm er in Kiel mit seinem Drachen teil und erreichte den 15. Platz.

ROYAL LEAGUE
Juan Carlos, the Olympic athlete: in 1972 he participated in Kiel with his dragon and finished 15th.

STRANDSEGLER
Josephine Charlotte von Belgien erfreut sich 1941 an der Nordsee bei De Panne.

LAND SAILING
1941, Josephine Charlotte of Belgium is happy to be at the North Sea near De Panne.

GEKRÖNTE HÄUPTER / CROWNED HEADS **23**

PARTYKAPITÄN
Hoheit Karim Aga Khan IV. nimmt 1968 Kurs auf das Jetset-Paradies Porto Cervo.

PARTY CAPTAIN
Highness Karim Aga Khan IV in 1968 setting course for the jet-set paradise of Porto Cervo.

PRIVATAUDIENZ
Kaiser Akihito rudert Ehefrau Michiko, Prinzessin Kiko und Prinz Hisahito durch die Sagami-Bucht. Das Bild ist eine Sensation, denn so privat sieht man den Tenno für gewöhnlich nie.

PRIVATE AUDIENCE
Emperor Akihito with his wife Michiko, Princess Kiko and Prince Hisahito rowing through the Sagami Bay. This picture is a sensation because you will usually never see the Tenno in such a private situation.

◀ **FAMILIENFEHDE**
König Georg V. bestimmt auf der »Britannia« den Kurs, während Wilhelm II. auf der »Meteor« auf Wind wartet. Der Wettstreit der segelnden Cousins untereinander hat die Beziehung zwischen England und Deutschland damals auf eine harte Probe gestellt.

FAMILY FEUD
King George V determines the direction on board the »Britannia« while William II is waiting for wind aboard the »Meteor«. At that time, the competition among the sailing cousins has put the relationship between England and Germany under a hard test.

KÖNIGIN ELISABETH II. und Prinz Philip empfangen 1953 vor den Fidschi-Inseln Gastgeschenke eines Häuptlings in Landestracht.

QUEEN ELIZABETH II and Prince Philip in 1953, receiving guest gifts from a chief wearing a national dress on the Fiji Islands.

Im 19. Jahrhundert war das Spiel mit Wind und Wellen zu einem elitären Sport der Könige geworden. Zur berühmten Cowes Week um die Isle of Wight, die als europäische Herrenregatta schlechthin galt, traten vor allem die Cousins König George V. von England, Kaiser Wilhelm II. und Zar Nikolaus II. von Russland gegeneinander an. Wobei: Segeln im sportlichen Sinne war das eigentlich nicht. Die majestätischen Yachten wurden nämlich von professionellen Skippern und Crews geführt, während die Durchlauchten dabeisaßen oder -standen, dann und wann das gekrönte Haupt schüttelten, kluge Ratschläge erteilten und nur mal für offizielle Postkartenmotive Hand ans Ruder legten.

Als besonders segelbegeistert galt dennoch der englische König. Seine Leidenschaft ging so weit, dass George V. als letzten Willen verfügte, seine geliebte Regattayacht »Britannia« möge doch bitte nach seinem Tod nahe der Isle of Wight versenkt werden – und so geschah es denn auch. Cousin Wilhelm, so heißt es in den Geschichtsbüchern, empfand das Ergebnis mancher Regatta vor der südenglischen Küste als Kränkung seiner selbst. Daher hatte der deutsche Kaiser schließlich mit der Kieler Woche in der Ostsee einfach seine eigenen Regatten protegiert.

In the 19th century playing with wind and waves had become an elite sport of kings. At famous Cowes Week around the Isle of Wight, which was par excellence as a European Men's Regatta, especially the cousins King George V of England, Emperor Wilhelm II and Czar Nicholas II of Russia competed against each other. However: It was not sailing in terms of sports. The majestic yachts were in fact led by professional skippers and crews, while the Serene Highnesses sat or stood there, now and then shaking their crowned heads, giving wise advice and touching the helm every now and then only for official postcard motifs.

The English King, however, was considered a particular sailing enthusiast. His passion was so huge that George V decreed as his last will that after his death his beloved racing yacht »Britannia« should be sunk near the Isle of Wight – and so it happened. Cousin William, as we read it in the history books, considered the results of some regattas off the Southern English coast an insult to himself. Therefore, the German Emperor had finally patronized the Kiel Week with his own regattas in the Baltic Sea.

GEKRÖNTE HÄUPTER / CROWNED HEADS 29

JÄGER & SAMMLER I
König Edward VIII. von England hatte zwei Laster – Yachten und verheiratete Frauen. Bilder, die ihn mit seiner neuesten Eroberung Wallis Simpson, einer zweifach geschiedenen bürgerlichen Amerikanerin, nackt plantschend vor der kroatischen Küste zeigten, zwangen ihn 1936 zum Thronverzicht.

HUNTERS & GATHERERS I
King Edward VIII of England had two vices – yachts and married women. Pictures showing him with his latest conquest Wallis Simpson, a twice divorced, middle-class American, splashing around wearing no clothes off the Croatian coast, forced him to abdicate in 1936.

◂ **JÄGER & SAMMLER II**
Den leidenschaftlichen Jäger, Trophäensammler und Dackelfan Philippe von Orléans brachte seine Yacht »Maroussia« 1901 bis nach Spitzbergen – nur das Packeis setzte seinem Drang nach Norden dort ein Ende.

HUNTERS & GATHERERS II
Philippe of Orléans, a keen hunter, trophy collector and Doxie fan made it to Spitzbergen on board his yacht »Maroussia« in 1901 – only the pack ice stopped his advance there.

EINSAM
Lady Di im Juli 1997 einsam und allein auf der »Jonikal« in der Bucht von Portofino. Doch der Eindruck täuscht, Diana war gar nicht einsam. Sie machte Liebesurlaub mit ihrem neuen Freund Dodi al Fayed, um sie herum standen Hunderte Fotografen. Wie einst Grace Kelly wusste auch Diana um die Macht der Bilder und wie man sie richtig inszenierte – das Bild der »traurigen Prinzessin« ging um die Welt.

LONELY
Lady Di in July of 1997, lonely and alone on board the »Jonikal« in the bay of the Portofino. However, this impression is deceptive, Diana wasn't alone at all. She was on love holidays with her new boyfriend Dodi al Fayed, there were hundreds of photographers around them. As once did Grace Kelly, Diana also knew the power of images and how to use them when properly staged – the image of the »sad princess« went around the world.

GEKRÖNTE HÄUPTER / CROWNED HEADS **31**

GEMEINSAM
Britische Kolonien und Protektorate bedeckten Ende des 19. Jahrhunderts gut ein Viertel der Erde. Kein Wunder, dass das Königshaus viel unterwegs sein musste, wenn es alle Überseegebiete besuchen wollte. Einsam und allein war dabei kein Monarch, wie dieses Bild von 1911 beweist: König George V., Königin Maria, Tochter Mary und Thronfolger Edward setzen von der »Britannia« an die Küste Irlands.

TOGETHER
By the end of the 19th century, British colonies and protectorates covered a good quarter of the earth. No wonder that the royal family had to be travelling a lot, if they wanted to visit all overseas territories. Not a monarch was lonely and alone then, as this picture from 1911 shows: King George V, Queen Mary, daughter Mary and heir Edward set off to Ireland aboard the »Britannia«.

DER 70. GEBURTSTAG
Norwegens Königin Sonja feierte 2007 ihren Geburtstag auf der »Norge« – und alle wollten mit ihr aufs Bild: Maria Teresa von Luxemburg, Henrik und Margrethe von Dänemark, Sonja und Harald von Norwegen, Silvia und Carl XVI. Gustaf von Schweden, Beatrix der Niederlande sitzen (v. l.). Mary und Frederik von Dänemark, Haakon und Mette-Marit von Norwegen, Victoria von Schweden, Philippe und Mathilde von Belgien müssen im Hintergrund stehen.

THE 70TH BIRTHDAY
In 2007 Norway's Queen Sonja celebrated her birthday on board the »Norge« – and everyone wanted to be with her on the picture: Maria Teresa of Luxembourg, Henrik and Margrethe of Denmark, Sonja and Harald of Norway, Silvia and Carl XVI Gustaf of Sweden, Beatrix of the Netherlands sitting (left to right). Mary and Frederik of Denmark, Haakon and Mette-Marit of Norway, Victoria of Sweden, Philippe and Mathilde of Belgium have to stand in the background.

ROYAL NAVY

(1) Victoria von Schweden erobert Hongkong vom Wasser aus. (2) Königin Sofia von Spanien mit Enkeln auf Mallorca. (3) Andrea Casiraghi fischt vor Ibiza eine Nixe aus dem Wasser. (4) Prinz William verteidigt beim Drachenbootrennen in Kanada die Krone. (5) Haakon von Norwegen und Mette-Marit landen im Hafen der Ehe. (6) Kate Middleton gibt den Drachen-Frauen auf der Themse die Richtung an. (7) Frederik und Mary von Dänemark müssen bei Eiseskälte in Grönland lustig winken. (8) Felipe von Spanien erzählt Ehefrau Letizia und den Töchtern Leonor und Sofia in Palma von seiner Segelregatta.

GEKRÖNTE HÄUPTER / CROWNED HEADS   **35**

ROYAL NAVY
(1) Victoria of Sweden conquering Hong Kong from the water. (2) Queen Sofia of Spain with grandchildren in Mallorca. (3) Andrea Casiraghi fishing a mermaid from the water at the coast of Ibiza. (4) Prince William defending the crown at the dragon boat race in Canada. (5) Haakon von Norway und Mette-Marit sailing to the harbour of marriage. (6) Kate Middleton indicating the direction to the dragon women on the River Thames. (7) Frederik and Mary of Denmark have to wave nicely in the freezing cold of Greenland. (8) Felipe of Spain telling his wife Letizia and his daughters Leonor and Sofia in Palma about his sailing regatta.

KÖNIG DER FISCHER
Carl Gustaf barfuß und in bunter Badehose auf Fischzug in den Schären, 1970.

THE FISHER KING
Carl Gustaf barefoot and in colourful swimsuit on fishing expedition in the archipelago in 1970.

OTTO VON BISMARCK
DEUTSCHER REICHSKANZLER
GERMAN REICHSKANZLER

»MEINE GEGNER WERFEN MIR OFT VOR, ICH STELLE DIE SEGEL NACH DEM WIND. ABER DARIN BESTEHT DOCH GERADE DIE KUNST DES SEGELNS!«

»MY OPPONENTS OFTEN ACCUSE ME OF SETTING THE SAILS TO THE WIND. HOWEVER, THIS IS JUST THE ART OF SAILING!«

GELDADEL
MONEY NOBILITY

Als den gekrönten Häuptern die Mittel ausgingen, legten sie ihre Yachten an die Kette und der Geldadel übernahm das Ruder. Ob Industriemagnate, Softwaregurus oder Tankerkönige, sie alle haben eins gemein — sie sind Meister im Fach der Selbstdarstellung.

As the crowned heads ran out of funds, they put their yachts on the lead and the financial aristocracy took over the helm. Whether tycoons, software gurus or tankship kings, they all have one thing in common — they are masters in the art of self-expression.

GEWINNER I
Larry Ellison, fünftreichster Mann der Welt, hat beim Segeln nur ein Ziel im Blick – den Sieg. Wie 2013 beim America's Cup, so auch hier am Steuer seiner »Sayonara«.

WINNER I
Larry Ellison, No 5 of the richest man man in the world, has only one goal in mind while sailing – victory. So he does at the America's Cup in 2013, and so he also does while steering his yacht »Sayonara«.

GEWINNER II Harold S. Vanderbilt in Action. Er verteidigt auf der »Ranger« den America's Cup gegen Angriffe der Europäer.
WINNER II Harold S. Vanderbilt in action. Aboard the »Ranger« he defends against attacking Europeans at the America's Cup.

Im beginnenden 20. Jahrhundert war der Segelsport in zwei Lager geteilt: Hier die auf Tradition pochenden Europäer. Dort amerikanische Millionäre, die mit ihren moderneren Yachten alle großen Regatten dominierten.
    Auf europäischer Seite stand Sir Thomas Lipton wie ein Fels in der Brandung. Der mit Tee reich gewordene Selfmademillionär irischer Abstammung liebte Segeln über alles. Die Schmach der Niederlage trug er stets mit Fassung, aufgeben aber wollte er nie. Zwischen 1899 und 1930 forderte er die Pokalhalter des America's Cup fünfmal heraus. Noch im hohen Alter von 80 Jahren schickte Lipton seine »Shamrock V« gegen die Ameri-

In the early 20th century, the sailing was divided into two camps: Here the Europeans insisting on tradition. There, American millionaires who dominated all the big regattas with their modern yachts. On the European side Sir Thomas Lipton stood solid as a rock. The self-made millionaire of Irish origin had become rich with tea amd loved sailing more than anything else. He always took the shame of defeat on the chin but he never wanted to give up. Between 1899 and 1930 he challenged the cup-holders of the America's Cup five times. Even at the age of 80, Lipton raced against the Americans on board the »Shamrock V«. Unfortunately he has never won any of the races, but at

BESTER VERLIERER Sir Thomas Lipton gibt auf der »Shamrock« wirklich alles, am Ende aber segelt der Mann mit dem Walrossbart Vanderbilt hinterher.
BEST LOSER Sir Thomas Lipton on board the »Shamrock« giving all he can but at the end the man with the walrus beard lags behind Vanderbilt.

kaner ins Rennen. Leider hat er keine der Regatten je gewonnen, was ihm am Ende aber wenigstens den Ehrenpreis als »Bester aller Verlierer« eingebracht hat. Einer seiner ewigen Widersacher war Harold S. Vanderbilt, dessen Großvater in den USA mit Eisenbahnen steinreich geworden war. Der Enkel nahm es mit dem Geldverdienen nicht so ernst. Während der Sommermonate kam er grundsätzlich nicht ins Büro, lieber war er jeden Tag auf dem Segelboot. Und so wird sein Name auch immer mit sportlichen Erfolgen verbunden bleiben. Harold S. Vanderbilt gewann den America's Cup dreimal. Auf einer seiner vielen Seereisen hat er übrigens dann auch Kontrakt-Bridge erfunden, die bis heute weltweit am häufigsten gespielte Variante des Kartenspiels.

least he was given the honorary prize as the »Best of all losers«. One of his eternal rival was Harold S. Vanderbilt, whose grandfather had become filthy rich with railroads in the United States. The grandson didn't take earning money too seriously. During the summer months, he never came to the office because he spent every day on the sailing boat. And therefore his name will always be associated with sporting success. Harold S. Vanderbilt won three times the America's Cup. On one of his many voyages he has by the way invented Contract Bridge which is the most widely played variation of the card game until today.

HERRENPROGRAMM
Harold S. Vanderbilt in der damals typischen, unter sportlichen Gesichtspunkten jedoch eher unvorteilhaften Segelkluft der 1930er-Jahre.

MEN'S PROGRAMME
Harold S. Vanderbilt in sailing uniform of the 1930s which was at that time typical but rather unfavourable in terms of sports.

DAMENPROGRAMM
Während Harold S. Vanderbilt das Ruder seiner »Ranger« führte, half seine Frau, die Yacht zu trimmen.

LADY'S PROGRAMME
While Harold S. Vanderbilt was holding the helm of his »Ranger«, his wife helped to trim the yacht.

COMPUTER-KRAKE
Paul Allens »Octopus« ist eine der zwölf größten Yachten der Welt. Wenn der Microsoft-Gründer zur Bordparty ruft, hat er stets ganz viele neue Freunde.

COMPUTER OCTOPUS
Paul Allen's »Octopus« is one of the twelve largest yachts in the world. Whenever the Microsoft founder calls for board party, he has quite a lot of new friends.

NECKERMANN-REISEN
Versandhauskönig Josef Neckermann 1986 mit Weltmeisterin Ulrike Deppe im Eiskanal der Olympia-Kanustrecke in Augsburg.

NECKERMANN REISEN
Mail order king Josef Neckermann in 1986 with world champion Ulrike Deppe in the ice channel of the Olympic canoe course in Augsburg.

POOL NIXE
Millionärin Ivana Trump stellt im Hafen von Cannes ihre Schätze zur Schau.

SWIMMING POOL MERMAID
Millionairess Ivana Trump showing off her treasures in the harbour of Cannes.

EINLADUNG
Wer mit Designer Roberto Cavalli in Saint Tropez die Nacht zum Tag machen will, muss barfuß kommen.

INVITATION
Whoever wants to turn night into day with designer Roberto Cavalli in St. Tropez has to be barefoot.

GELDADEL / MONEY NOBILITY **48**

GRIECHISCHE TRAGÖDIE ▶
Während Athina Onassis 1958 am Pool der »Christina O.« die Beine baumeln lässt, erobert ihr Mann an Deck Maria Callas.

GREEK TRAGEDY
While Athina Onassis is dangling her legs at the pool of the »Christina O.« in 1958, her husband conquers Maria Callas on deck.

VICTORY
Englands ehemaliger Premier Sir Winston Churchill eroberte als Dauersommergast auf Onassis' Yacht 1959 Marokko.

VICTORY
Being a permanent summer guest on Onassis' yacht England's former Prime Minister Sir Winston Churchill conquered Morocco in 1959.

Der Yachthafen von Monte Carlo wurde dank Aristoteles Onassis zur größten Freilichtbühne der Welt. Hier sitzt man wie auf dem Präsentierteller, während das Publikum auf den Hügeln drumherum applaudiert. Genau das war es, was der kleine Grieche mit der großen Yacht besonders genoss. Seine »Christina O.« bot 16 Gästen und 40 Mann Besatzung Platz, auf dem Oberdeck stand ein gelbes Wasserflugzeug, die Barhocker in Aris Bar waren mit Walpenishaut bezogen, der Boden des Pools konnte hoch- und runtergefahren werden, was Dauergast Winston Churchill größtes Vergnügen bereitete. Sein Lieblingsbrot ließ sich Onassis täglich aus Paris, Orangen aus Griechenland einfliegen. Zu Onassis' Gästen zählten neben dem Fürstenpaar unter anderem Marilyn Monroe, Frank Sinatra, Elizabeth Taylor, Richard Burton und Eva Peron. Schlagzeilen machte Onassis aber vor allem mit glamourösen Abenteuern: Mit der Operndiva Maria Callas lag er im Bett, während ihr Mann auf Deck in der Sonne döste und seine eigene Frau Athina im Pool war. Auf der »Christina O.« eroberte er auch später Jackie Kennedy, die Witwe des ermordeten US-amerikanischen Präsidenten, die er 1968 heiratete.

Thanks to Aristoteles Onassis the yachting port of Monte Carlo became the largest outdoor theatre in the world. Here one sits like on display while the audience on the hills is applauding. This was exactly what the little Greek particularly enjoyed on the large yacht. His »Christina O.« offered space for 16 guests and 40 crew members, on the upper deck there was a yellow waterplane, the bar stools in Aris bar were covered with whale penis skin, the bottom of the pool could be lifted and lowered, which gave the greatest pleasure to permanent guest Winston Churchill. Every day, Onassis had his favourite bread flown in from Paris and the oranges from Greece. Besides the Royal Couple, Onassis also had guests like Marilyn Monroe, Frank Sinatra, Elizabeth Taylor, Richard Burton and Eva Peron. However, Onassis made headlines especially with glamorous adventures: he was in bed with opera diva Maria Callas, while her husband was dozing on deck in the sun and his own wife Athina was in the pool. On board the »Christina O.« he later also conquered Jackie Kennedy, the widow of the assassinated U.S. President, and married her in 1968.

GROSSE FRAUEN hatten es Onassis angetan, ob Operndiva Maria Callas (oben) oder Jacqueline Kennedy.

GREAT WOMEN was what Onassis liked, be it diva Maria Callas (above) or Jacqueline Kennedy.

◀ **KLEINER MANN**
Aristoteles Onassis empfing auf seiner Yacht gern Gäste. Darunter auch den Playboy Porfirio Rubirosa (rechts), der im Ruf stand, 235 Lebensgefährtinnen gehabt zu haben.

LITTLE MAN
Aristoteles Onassis loved receiving guests onboard his yacht. Including the Playboy Porfirio Rubirosa (on the right), who was said to have had 235 partners in life.

RAUBFISCH
Al Capone genießt 1930 die Freiheit bei Fisch und Zigarre. Kurz zuvor war der berüchtigte Mafiaboss von Chicago wegen guter Führung nach nur zehn Monaten aus dem Gefängnis entlassen worden.

PREDATORY FISH
Al Capone enjoying freedom in 1930, while having fish and a cigar. Shortly before, the notorious mafia boss of Chicago had been released from prison for good behaviour after only ten months.

GOLDFISCH
Sir Bernard Dudley Frank Docker war in den 1960er-Jahren einer der reichsten Briten. Hier steuern der Industrielle und Gattin Norah, eine ehemalige Nachtclub-Tänzerin, ihre Yacht »Shemara« die Themse hinauf. Das Paar wurde ob seines überbordenden Lebensstils kritisiert.

GOLDFISH
In the 1960s, Sir Bernard Dudley Frank Docker was one of Britain's richest men. The industrialist and his wife Norah, a former nightclub dancer, steering their yacht »Shemara« up the River Thames. The couple was often criticized for their lifestyle.

SILBERFISCH
Millionär Richard Branson albert bei einem Fotoshooting für seine Fluglinie Virgin mit Top-Model Karolina Kurkova herum.

SILVERFISH
Millionaire Richard Branson fooling around with supermodel Karolina Kurkova during a photo shoot for his airline Virgin.

WILLIAM SOMERSET MAUGHAM,
SCHRIFTSTELLER
WRITER

»MONACO IST EIN LICHTER ORT MIT ZWIELICHTIGEN MENSCHEN.«

»MONACO IS A BRIGHT PLACE WITH SHADY PEOPLE.«

REICH UND SCHÖN
WEALTHY AND BEAUTIFUL

In den 1950er-Jahren übernahmen Stars und Sternchen das Ruder an der Côte d'Azur. Designer, Models, Sänger und Schauspieler, mit Schönheit und noch mehr Geld gesegnet, gaben den Fotografen Futter.

In the 1950s stars and starlets took over at the Côte d'Azur. Designers, models, singers and actors, blessed with beauty and even more money, made the photographers happy.

DIVA UND RIVA I
Eine Riva gehört seit den 1960er-Jahren zur Grundausstattung der Playboys, genauso wie eine schöne Frau an der Seite. Gunter Sachs hatte beides – Boot und Brigitte Bardot.

DIVA AND RIVA I
Since the 1960s, a Riva has been part of the playboys' basic equipment, as does a beautiful woman at their side. Gunter Sachs had them both – the boat and Brigitte Bardot.

REICH UND SCHÖN / WEALTHY AND BEAUTIFUL 58

MODEL, SCHAUSPIELERIN UND SEXSYMBOL Brigitte Bardot machte den Bikini populär, das verschlafene Fischernest St. Tropez bekannt und die Männer reihenweise verrückt.

MODEL, ACTRESS AND SEX SYMBOL Brigitte Bardot made the bikini popular, the sleepy fishing village St. Tropez known and drove every man crazy.

TRAUMPAAR ▶
Gunter Sachs war ein Meister der Selbstdarstellung. Auch die Flitterwochen mit Brigitte Bardot auf Tahiti 1966 waren von ihm in Szene gesetzt, ein Fotograf stets zur Stelle.

PERFECT COUPLE
Gunter Sachs used to be a master of self-promotion. In 1966, he even put the honeymoon with Brigitte Bardot on Tahiti in the limelight – a photographer was never far away.

Zwei Namen genügen, um eine ganze Ära zu beschreiben – Brigitte Bardot und Gunter Sachs. Die französische Schauspielerin und der deutsche Lebemann, das Traumpaar der 1960er-Jahre an der Côte d'Azur. Hier liebten, fetzten und versöhnten sie sich, hier ließ der reiche Erbe 1000 rote Rosen aus einem Helikopter regnen, hier verführte er seine Braut in einer Mondnacht auf dem sanft schaukelnden Heck einer Riva Aquarama. Ihr Lebensmotto war »dolce far niente« – das süße Nichtstun –, die perfekte Kulisse dazu St. Tropez. Doch ihre Liebe war vergänglich. Einen Playboy wie Gunter Sachs zu halten, war nicht einmal einer Ikone möglich. Und so scheiterte ihre Ehe nur drei Jahre, nachdem Sachs ihr im offenen Hemd und barfuß in Las Vegas vor den Traualtar ewige Treue geschworen hatte. Denn treu war er offensichtlich nicht. »Ich hatte nicht einen Mann allein geheiratet, sondern eine ganze Sippschaft herumscharwenzelnder Playboys, die durch eine Komplizenschaft enger zusammengeschmiedet waren, als unsere Ehe es vermochte. Sie suchten sich schöne, junge und vorzugsweise dumme Gefährtinnen«, sagte Brigitte Bardot später in einem Interview. »Da ich die letztgenannte Qualifikation aber nicht besaß, fiel ich Gunter zunehmend lästig.« Die Folge: »Er playboyte herum, und ich stand ihm dabei im Weg ...«

Two names suffice to describe a whole era – Brigitte Bardot and Gunter Sachs. The French actress and the German bon vivant, the dream couple of the 60s on the Côte d'Azur. They loved each other, argued and reconciled just here, here the rich heir let the sky rain 1,000 red roses from a helicopter, here he seduced his wife in a moonlit night on the gently swaying back of a Riva Aquarama. Their motto was »dolce far niente« – sweet idleness –, with St. Tropez as the perfect backdrop. But their love was finite. Even an icon was not able to hold a playboy like Gunter Sachs. And so their marriage failed only three years after Sachs had sworn eternal fidelity to BB while standing barefoot and with an open shirt in front of the altar in Las Vegas. He was obviously not faithful to her. »I didn't marry just one man, but a whole clan of restless playboys whose complicity was tighter than our marriage could be. They were looking for beautiful, young and preferably foolish partners«, Brigitte Bardot said during an interview. »Since I didn't qualify for the latter, I more and more inconvenienced Gunter.« The consequence: »He went on playing his playboy role and I stood in his way...«

SEITENSPRUNG
John Hurt und Julie Christie leihen sich 1969 in einer Drehpause ein Motorboot.

ESCAPADE
John Hurt and Julie Christie borrow a motorboat during a filming break in 1969.

ABSPRUNG ▶
Als Liebhaber von Stephanie von Monaco machte Jean-Yves Le Fur eine gute Figur. Beim Absprung von Bord eher weniger: Nase zu und rein ...

JUMP
Jean-Yves Le Fur made a good impression as Stephanie of Monaco's lover. But now when jumping overboard, he looks less good: The nose held closed and off into the water...

KRIMIKÖNIG
Der Fotograf hatte den Regisseur lange zu diesem Bild vor der Kulisse von Cannes überreden müssen. Alfred Hitchcock kommentiert es mit brummiger Miene.

THRILLER KING
The photographer had long persuaded the director for this picture in front of the backdrop of Cannes. Alfred Hitchcock comments it with a grumpy face.

KLATSCHTANTE
Elsa Maxwell war die erste Klatschreporterin von Hollywood. In Venedig veranstaltete sie Bootsrennen für reiche Europäer, und in Monaco verkuppelte sie Onassis mit Maria Callas.

CHATTERBOX
Elsa Maxwell was the first yellow press reporter of Hollywood. She organised boat races for rich Europeans in Venice and in Monaco she paired off Onassis with Maria Callas.

WATERLOO
Björn, Agnetha und Anni-Frid albern auf Bennys Boot rum. Der Abba-Gründer (mit Wasserpistole) steuerte auch die Segelyacht im Musikvideo zu »Knowing Me, Knowing You«, während die anderen seekrank wurden.

WATERLOO
Björn, Agnetha and Anni-Frid kidding around on Benny's boat. The founder of ABBA (with water pistol) also steered the sailing yacht in the music video »Knowing Me, Knowing You« while the others got seasick.

WASSERBETT
Curd Jürgens besaß Villen an der Côte d'Azur und auf den Bahamas – und ein Bett am Strand von Mauritius. Hier liegt er wie ein gestrandeter Wal. »Wo er hintrat, wuchs Futter für Society-Kolumnisten«, schrieb das Magazin »Der Spiegel« damals über den »normannischer Schrank« Curd Jürgens.

WATERBED
Curd Juergens had villas on the Côte d'Azur and on the Bahamas – and a bed on the beach of Mauritius. Here he lies like a stranded whale. »Wherever he was going, there was ›food‹ for the society columnists«, the Spiegel magazine wrote about the »Norman giant« Curd Jürgens.

DER GROSSE DIKTATOR macht Kerze. Charlie Chaplin 1933 auf der Yacht seines Freundes Joseph Schenck. Chaplin selbst besaß zwei Boote.

THE GREAT DICTATOR performing a shoulder stand. Charlie Chaplin aboard the yacht of his friend Joseph Schenck in 1933. Chaplin himself was the owner of two boats.

REICH UND SCHÖN / WEALTHY AND BEAUTIFUL 69

STEUERMANN
George C ooney steuert den Chauffeur eines Wassertaxis an den Ohren durch Venedig.

HELMSMAN
George C ooney steering the chauffeur of a water taxi through Venice by his ears.

◀ **DIVA UND RIVA II**
Audrey Hepburn bei einem privaten Bootsausflug auf einem Schweizer See 1950.

DIVA AND RIVA II
Audrey Hepburn on a private boat trip on a Swiss lake in 1950.

REICH UND SCHÖN / WEALTHY AND BEAUTIFUL **70**

POP ART
Andy Warhol 1990 auf großer Fahrt im See des New Yorker Central Parks.

POP ART
1990, Andy Warhol on his big cruise on the lake of the Central Park in New York.

POP STAR
Madonna mit Freund Jesus Luz und Adoptivkindern David Banda Mwale und Mercy James 2009 in Portofino.

POP STAR
Madonna and her boyfriend Jesus Luz and the adopted children David Banda Mwale and Mercy James in 2009 in Portofino.

REICH UND SCHÖN / WEALTHY AND BEAUTIFUL 73

SZENEN EINER EHE Richard Burton und Elizabeth Taylor 1968 auf der »Kalisma« – mit Pekinesen, Yorkshire Terrier und Clint Eastwood (rechts).

SCENES FROM A MARRIAGE Richard Burton and Elizabeth Taylor in 1968 aboard the Kalizma – with Pekinese dog, Yorkshire Terrier and Clint Eastwood (on the right).

In Monte Carlo kam es in den 1950er- und 1960er-Jahren zum Society-Showdown. Auf engstem Raum trafen Elizabeth Taylor und Richard Burton, Aristoteles Onassis und das monegassische Fürstenpaar aufeinander – und jeder proklamierte für sich, im Mittelpunkt des Interesses zu stehen. Die Strahlkraft einer Yacht auf das eigene Ansehen hatten Burton und Taylor auf einer Party in Cannes erlebt und sich dann die Motoryacht »Kalizma« gekauft. Sie machten sie mit Gemälden von Degas, Picasso und van Gogh zu einem schwimmenden Museum. Kostbarstes Stück an Bord war jedoch der 69,4 Karat schwere Diamant Taylor/Burton, den Richard Burton für 1,2 Millionen Dollar als Zeichen seiner Liebe gekauft hatte. In dieser Umgebung also lebten sie mit fünf Kindern aus fünf Ehen, einer gemeinsamen Adoptivtochter, einem Pekinesen und zwei Yorkshire Terriern. »Wir sind ein liebenswertes, charmantes, dekadentes, hoffnungsloses Paar«, sagte Burton, und Elizabeth Taylor fügte hinzu: »Alle bezahlen hier Eintritt, um Liz und Dick zu sehen. Und wir zeigen ihnen, was sie wollen ...«

In the 1950s and 1960s Monte Carlo was the stage for society showdowns. Elizabeth Taylor and Richard Burton, Aristoteles Onassis and the Monegasque royal couple met each other in confined spaces – and each of them proclaimed to be the centre of attention. At a party in Cannes Burton and Taylor experienced the charisma a yacht would give to their own reputation and then they bought the motor yacht »Kalizma«. With paintings by Degas, Picasso and van Gogh they made it a swimming museum. However, the most precious piece on board was the 69.4 carat diamond Taylor/Burton Richard Burton had bought for 1.2 million Dollars as a proof of his love. In this surrounding they lived with five children from five marriages, their adopted daughter, one Pekinese dog and two Yorkshire Terriers. »We are a lovely, charming, decadent, hopeless couple«, Burton said and Elizabeth Taylor added: »They all pay admission here to see Liz and Dick. And we show them what they want...«

VORSPIEL
Der große Chansonnier und Verführer Charles Aznavour gibt sich redlich Mühe, doch seine Begleiterinnen interessiert sein Vorspiel gar nicht.

FORETASTE
The great composer and seducer Charles Aznavour going to great lengths, but his companions aren't interested in foreplay at all.

TROCKENÜBUNG
Roger Federer versucht sich auf den Bahamas als waghalsiger Segler, hängt sich richtig rein, während der Bug des Katamarans fest auf Land liegt ...

DRY RUN
Roger Federer on the Bahamas trying to be a daring sailor, breaking his neck to do so, while the bow of the catamaran rests firmly on land...

FRAUENSCHWARM ▶
Errol Flynn mit Ehefrau Lili Damita 1940
an Bord seiner geliebten Yacht »Zaca«.

HEARTBREAKER
Errol Flynn with his wife Lili Damita in
1940 onboard his beloved Yacht »Zaca«.

Errol Flynn war auf einem Schiff gezeugt worden, in einem Hafen zur Welt gekommen, als Sohn eines Meeresbiologen am Wasser aufgewachsen und als Skipper seines ersten eigenen Bootes von einem Filmproduzenten für Hollywood entdeckt worden. Und so spielte Flynn in mehr als 60 Filmen (»Herr der sieben Meere«) auch stets das, was er von Herzen war – ein Abenteurer, der mit nacktem Oberkörper und stolzer Brust am Ruder eines Schiffes den Naturgewalten trotzt. Im Jahre 1945 aber befand sich Flynn in einer tiefen Sinnkrise. Und da tat er, was Abenteurer in so einer Situation eben tun: »Anstatt mich umzubringen oder mich hemmungslos zu betrinken, habe ich mir ein Boot gekauft. Denn die See ist meine einzig wahre Liebe.« Fortan lebte Flynn auf dem Zweimaster »Zaca«. Auf der Flucht vor US-Steuerfahndern verschlug es ihn zunächst nach Mallorca und weiter nach Monaco. Als die Polizei dort dann gegen ihn wegen Unzucht an Bord ermittelte, ging Flynn für einige Jahre in Port Antonio auf Jamaika vor Anker. Und auch sein Tod 1959 steht in Zusammenhang mit der geliebten »Zaca«: An dem Tag nämlich, als Flynn sie aus Geldnot verkaufen musste, erlitt er einen Herzinfarkt und starb.

Errol Flynn was conceived on a ship, he was given birth in a port, he raised as a son of a marine biologist next to the water and was discovered as skipper of his own first boat by a movie producer in Hollywood. And so Flynn played in more than 60 movies (»Legend of the seven seas«) always a character he actually was from the heart – an adventurer at the helm of a ship withstanding the forces of nature with bare and proud chest. However, in the year 1945, Flynn had a deep crisis of meaning. And there he did what adventurers just do in such a situation: »Instead of killing myself or getting unrestrainedly drunk, I bought myself a boat. After all the sea is my only true love.« From then Flynn lived aboard the two-master »Zaca«. The escape from U.S. tax investigators took first him to Mallorca and then to Monaco. When the police investigated against him for sexual immorality on board, Flynn dropped anchor at Port Antonio on Jamaica for some years. And even his death in 1959 is linked to his much loved »Zaca«: The day Flynn had to sell her in need of money, he had a heart attack and died.

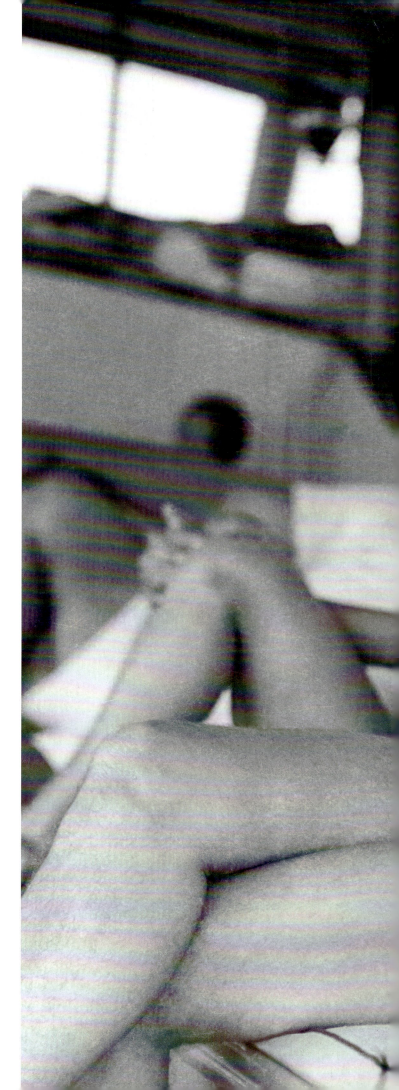

REICH UND SCHÖN / WEALTHY AND BEAUTIFUL 78

STARPARADE
(1) Mit der Lizenz zum Grüßen – Pierce Brosnan und Trine Dyrholm. (2) Elton John begibt sich auf schwankendes Terrain. (3) Bono mit Helena Christensen und Penelope Cruz – seine Frau fand das Foto gar nicht schön. (4) Alle Jahre wieder Medienrummel um Millionär Bram van Leeuwen. (5) Und wo ein Millionär oder Prinz ist, da darf auch Ira von Fürstenberg nicht fehlen. (6) Böser Fauxpas: Rod Stewart und Penny Lancaster – mit High Heels an Bord. (7) Will Smith, Angelina Jolie und Jack Black quälen einen Plastikhai. (8) P. Diddy und Bruce Willis ganz cool, Mann.

STAR PARADE

(1) With the license to greet – Pierce Brosnan and Trine Dyrholm. (2) Elton John setting out on swaying terrain. (3) Bono with Helena Christensen and Penelope Cruz – his wife did not like that photo at all. (4) The every year media hype about millionaire Bram van Leeuwen. (5) And where there is a millionaire or a prince, also Ira of Fuerstenberg should not be missing. (6) Nasty faux pas: Rod Stewart and Penny Lancaster – with high heels on board. (7) Will Smith, Angelina Jolie and Jack Black tormenting a toy shark. (8) P. Diddy and Bruce Willis absoulutely cool, man.

VERLOBUNG
Auf einem Ruderboot auf dem Luganer See geben Romy Schneider und Alain Delon 1959 ihre Verlobung bekannt. Viereinhalb Jahre später sind sie immer noch verlobt. Erst als Romy Schneider 1963 in Amerika die Komödie »Leih mir deinen Mann« dreht und Delon zu Hause eine andere küsst, ist Schluss.

ENGAGEMENT
On a rowboat on Lake Lugano Romy Schneider and Alain Delon announced their engagement in 1959. Four and a half years later they are still engaged. It was over only when Delon was kissing someone else at home while Romy Schneider was in America shooting the comedy »Lend me your husband« in 1963.

REICH UND SCHÖN / WEALTHY AND BEAUTIFUL **82**

FREIES KUBA
Diego Maradona erholt sich im Jahre 2000 auf einem Segeltörn vor Kuba von den Strapazen einer Entziehungskur.

FREE CUBA
On a sailing trip around Cuba in 2000, Diego Maradona recovers from the rigours of a detoxification.

FREIER FALL ▶
Designer Stefano Gabbana
geht vor Portofino baden.

FREE FALL
Designer Stefano Gabbana goes
swimming at Portofino.

HAUPTROLLE
Humphrey Bogart liebte das Segeln. Hier takelt er seinen Albatross für eine Regatta des Newport Yacht Clubs auf.

LEADING PART
Humphrey Bogart loved sailing. Here he rigs up his Albatross/dinghy for a regatta of the Newport Yacht Club.

GASTSPIEL
Die göttliche Greta Garbo liebte Seereisen und war oft zu Gast auf Onassis' Yacht »Christina O.«.

AWAY GAME
The divine Greta Garbo loved sea trips and was a frequent guest on Onassis' yacht »Christina O.«.

MUSIKDAMPFER I
Die Beatles stechen 1964 mit der »Southern Trail« von Miami in See. Als Paul McCartney dann auf dem Ausflugsdampfer ein Klavier entdeckt, setzt er sich spontan ran und gibt der Crew ein exklusives Solokonzert.

MUSIC STEAMER I
The Beatles put to see from Miami on board the »Southern Trail« in 1964. When Paul McCartney then discovered a piano on board the excursion steamer, he spontaneously performed an exclusive solo concert for the crew.

REICH UND SCHÖN / WEALTHY AND BEAUTIFUL **87**

MUSIKDAMPFER II
Die Rolling Stones präsentierten auf dem Hudson River in New York 1966 ihr Album »Aftermath« – und legten danach erst einmal die Füße hoch.

MUSIC STEAMER II
In 1966 the Rolling Stones presented their album »Aftermath« on the Hudson River in New York – and then put their feet up.

GALLIONSFIGUR
Pamela Anderson gehört heute zum Inventar der Côte d'Azur.

FIGUREHEAD
Today, Pamela Anderson is part of the inventory of the Côte d'Azur.

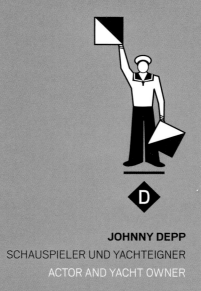

JOHNNY DEPP
SCHAUSPIELER UND YACHTEIGNER
ACTOR AND YACHT OWNER

»MIT GELD KANN
MAN KEIN GLÜCK KAUFEN.
ABER EINE YACHT, MIT
DER MAN INS GLÜCK
SEGELN KANN.«

»YOU CANNOT BUY
HAPPINESS WITH MONEY,
HOWEVER, YOU CAN BUY
A YACHT YOU CAN SAIL
INTO HAPPINESS WITH.«

YACHTFREUNDE
Der Komponist Giacomo Puccini 1908 am Steuer der »Cic Cic San«. Links sitzt sein Freund, der Autohersteller Tito Ricordi.

YACHTING FRIENDS
The composer Giacomo Puccini in 1908 at the helm of »Cic Cic San«. His friend and car maker Tito Ricordi sitting to his left.

KLUGE KÖPFE

Was haben Einstein, Ghandi, Kennedy und Putin gemein? Sie alle haben es stets verstanden, sich auf dem Wasser von ihrer besten Seite zu zeigen — als Casanova, Pilger, Sunnyboy oder toller Hecht.

SMART MINDS

What do Einstein, Gandhi, Kennedy and Putin have in common? They all have always succeeded in showing up on the water at their best — as Casanova, pilgrim, sunnyboy or cool pike.

KLUGE KÖPFE / SMART MINDS **92**

CASANOVA EINSTEIN ▶
In jedem Hafen eine Braut –
Albert Einstein mit einer »Freundin«
1930 auf der Havel.

EINSTEIN, THE CASANOVA
A chick in every port –
Albert Einstein with a »girlfriend«
on the Havel in 1930.

SUNNYBOY EINSTEIN
Im Jahre 1932 emigrierte Einstein in die USA, seinen geliebten Jollenkreuzer musste er in Deutschland zurücklassen. Das Foto zeigt ihn 1945 mit einem geliehenen Boot in Saranac Lake, New York.

EINSTEIN, THE SUNNYBOY
In 1932, Einstein emigrated to the United States, he had to leave his beloved dinghy cruiser back in Germany. The photo shows him in 1945 with a borrowed boot in Saranac Lake, New York.

Albert Einsteins Forschungen zur Struktur von Materie, Raum und Zeit sowie dem Wesen der Gravitation veränderten unser physikalisches Weltbild. Wer aber denkt, der bekannteste Physiker aller Zeiten wäre nur ein rationaler Kopfmensch gewesen, der irrt sich. Einsteins große Leidenschaft galt seinem »Tümmler«, den er liebevoll »mein dickes Segelschiff« nannte. Er lag in Caputh, am Ufer des Schwielowsees, an dem Einstein von 1929 bis 1932 ein Sommerhaus besaß. In der Kajüte gab es zwei Schlafplätze, einen Tisch für vier Personen, einen versenkbaren Kocher und eine Toilette. Hier konnte er in Ruhe nachdenken und philosophieren, hierher zog er sich gern mit weiblichem Besuch zurück, von dem seine Frau Elsa nichts wissen durfte, und hier erläuterte der Freizeitskipper Freunden seine neuesten physikalischen Theorien. Dabei fiel ihnen auf, wie der Nobelpreisträger an Bord aufblühte: »Er führt das Boot mit der Geschicklichkeit und Furchtlosigkeit eines Knaben. Er hisst die Segel selbst, klettert im Boot herum, um Taue und Leinen zu straffen, und hantiert mit Stangen und Haken, um das Boot vom Ufer abzulegen. Das Vergnügen an dieser Beschäftigung spiegelt sein Antlitz, es klingt in seinen Worten und in seinem glücklichen Lachen wider.«

Albert Einstein's studies of the structure of matter, space and time and the nature of gravity changed our physical world view. But anyone who thinks the most famous physicist of all time would have been a rational analytic person is mistaken. Einstein's great passion was his »Tümmler«, which he lovingly called »my thick sailing ship.« It was kept in Caputh, on the shore of Lake Schwielow, where Einstein owned a summer residence from 1929 to 1932. In the cabin there were two beds, a table for four people, a retractable cooker and a toilet. Here he could reflect and philosophise in peace, here he liked to retreat with his female visit, of which his wife Elsa wasn't supposed to know anything, and here the leisure skipper explained his friends his latest physical theories. Here they noticed how the Nobel Prize winner thrived on board: »He leads the boat with the skills and fearlessness of a boy. He hoists the sails himself, climbing around in the boat to tighten ropes, and is busy with rods and hooks to cast the boat off the shore. The pleasure of this activity reflects in his face, it echoes in his words and his happy laughter.«

BABY AN BORD
Der walisische Dichter Dylan Thomas (links) und seine Frau Caitlin wohnten mit ihren drei Kindern in einem Bootshaus. Das Foto zeigt sie 1950 bei einem Ausflug mit einem Fischer.

BABY ON BOARD
The Welsh poet Dylan Thomas (left) and his wife Caitlin lived with their three children in a boathouse. The photo shows them on a trip with a fisherman in 1950.

REISEGRUPPE GANDHI

Im Jahre 1931 brach Mahatma Gandhi in Indien an Bord der »SS Rajputana« nach England auf, um dort über Indiens Unabhängigkeit zu verhandeln. Während der wochenlangen Reise saß er oft an Deck und schrieb. Zu seinen Füßen schlief seine Schülerin und Assistentin Madeleine Slade. Foto rechts: Gandhi betritt in Folkestone britischen Boden, warme Kleidung im Arm.

TRAVEL PARTY GANDHI

In 1931, Mahatma Gandhi started in India on board the »SS Rajputana« heading for England to conduct negotiations on India's independence there. During the week-long trip, he often sat on the deck and wrote. His student and assistant Madeleine Slade slept at his feet. Right photo: Gandhi stepping onto British soil in Folkestone, carrying warm clothes.

FOTOGEN I
Fotos von John F. Kennedy beim Segeln waren Teil einer ausgefeilten PR-Strategie. Sie sollten das Image des sportlichen, anpackenden Politikers festigen. Ob beim Windspiel mit Jacqueline 1953 oder beim Ausflug mit Tochter Caroline 1963 – Fotografen hielten jeden Augenblick fest.

PHOTOGENIC I
Photos of John F. Kennedy sailing were part of an elaborate PR strategy. They were supposed to consolidate the image of the sporty, tackling politician. Whether at the game with the wind with Jacqueline 1953 or on a trip with daughter Caroline 1963 – Photographers captured every moment.

Kein Politiker der Welt verstand es je besser, sich auf Fotos ins rechte Licht zu setzen, als John F. Kennedy. Seine Lieblingskulisse war dabei stets ein Boot, oder besser gesagt: sein Boot. Kennedys Eltern besaßen ein Sommerhaus am Strand von Cape Cod, zu seinem 15. Geburtstag bekam der Junior den gaffelgetakelten Daysailer »Victura« geschenkt, mit dem er später auch als Kongressmitglied, als Senator und als Präsident der Vereinigten Staaten von Amerika segelte. Seiner Verlobten Jacqueline Bouvier brachte er an Bord der »Victura« das Segeln bei – natürlich war ein Fotograf dabei. Das Porträt in der Zeitschrift »Life« zeigte das verliebte Paar dann auf dem Vordeck und beim Auftakeln. Für eine andere Reportage setze sich das Ehepaar Kennedy mit Kindern an Bord des Daysailers in Szene. Bilder wie diese passten zum Image des Präsidenten als smartem, vitalem Sunnyboy. Zugleich kaschierten sie, dass Kennedy gesundheitliche Probleme hatte und wegen eines Rückenleidens ein Korsett tragen musste.

No politician in the world knew better how to show himself in a favourable light on photos than John F. Kennedy. His favourite scene was always a boat, or better still: his boat. Kennedy's parents owned a summer residence at the beach of Cape Cod. On his 15th birthday, he received the gaff rigged daysailer »Victura« as a present, which he later also used for sailing as Congressman, as Senator and as President of the United States. On board the »Victura« he taught his fiancée Jacqueline Bouvier how to sail – of course, a photographer was there, too. The portrait in the Life magazine then showed the couple in love on the foredeck and while rigging. For another documentary, the couple Kennedy put themselves with their children in the limelight on board the daysailer. Images like these matched the image of the president as a smart, vital sunnyboy. At the same time they concealed the fact that Kennedy had health problems and had to wear a corset.

FOTOGEN II
Zweimal Kennedy, zweimal an Bord: 1963 als smarter US-Präsident bei der Zeitungslektüre auf der Präsidentenyacht »Honey Fitz« und frisch verliebt mit Jacqueline auf seiner »Victura«.

PHOTOGENIC II
Twice Kennedy, twice on board: 1963 as smart US President while reading the newspaper onboard the Presidential yacht »Honey Fitz« and newly in love with Jacqueline on his »Victura«.

FAHRT INS BLAUE
Barack Obama schätzt festen Boden unter den Füßen. Es sei denn, schwankender Untergrund dient einem guten Zweck, wie hier mit Ehefrau Michelle und Tochter Sasha auf der »Bay Point Lady«. Der US-Präsident demonstrierte damit nach der Explosion der Ölplattform Deepwater Horizon für die Schönheit der Ferienregion am Golf von Mexiko. Später plantschte er auch noch fotogen im blauen Wasser.

OUT IN THE BLUE
Barack Obama appreciates solid ground under his feet. Unless it serves a good purpose, like here with wife Michelle and daughter Sasha onboard the »Bay Point Lady«. After the explosion of the oil platform Deepwater Horizon, the US President used it to demonstrate for the beauty of the holiday region in the Gulf of Mexico. Later, he also splashed photogenically in blue water.

KLUGE KÖPFE / SMART MINDS **103**

FISCH & VIPS
Wenn zwei eingefleischte Texaner das Schießeisen beiseite legen und sich aufs Wasser begeben, dann muss das einen Grund haben. Böse Zungen behaupteten 2003, US-Präsident George W. Bush (rechts) musste gerade mal wieder sein Image aufpolieren, als er sich mit Vater George vor Maine zum Angeln traf.

FISH & VIP'S
If two diehard Texans put their shooting irons aside and set out on the water, then must be a reason. Malicious tongues claimed in 2003 that US President George W. Bush (right) had to bolster his image when he met with his father George off the coast of Maine for fishing.

VORSCHOTER
Franklin Roosevelt war der erste US-Präsident, der das Segeln öffentlich zelebrierte – mit Krawatte.

BOWMAN
Franklin Roosevelt was the first U.S. President to publicly celebrate sailing – with tie.

TOLLER HECHT
Im Finnischen Meerbusen tauchte Wladimir Putin im Juli 2013 mit einem Mini-U-Boot in 60 Meter Tiefe ab, um das Wrack der 1869 gesunkenen »Oleg« zu inspizieren. Elf Tage später tauchte er in Sibirien mit Verteidigungsminister Sergei Shoigu wieder auf.

COOL PIKE
In July of 2013, Vladimir Putin dived down onboard a mini submarine to a depth of 60 metres in the Gulf of Finland in order to examine the wreck of the »Oleg« that sunk in 1869. Eleven days later, he emerged in Siberia with Secretary of Defence Sergei Shoigu.

UNTERSEE-ABENTEURER
Jacques Piccard war einer der bedeutendsten Tiefseeforscher der Welt. So gelang es ihm zum Beispiel, im Marianengraben 10 916 Meter tief zu tauchen. Weniger spektakulär waren seine Testfahrten mit dem Tauchboot »F. A. Forel« hier im Königssee. »Es ist, wie wenn man bei Nacht und dichtem Nebel über dem Boden der Sahara dahinschwebt.«

UNDERWATER ADVENTURER
Jacques Piccard was one of the most important deep sea researchers in the world. He succeeded, for example, to dive 10,916 metres deep in the Mariana Trench. His test dives with the submersible »F. A. Forel« here in the Lake Königssee were less spectacular. »It's like hovering over the Sahara at night and with thick fog.«

SKIPPER SCHMIDT

Der Brahmsee war ein unscheinbares Gewässer in Schleswig-Holstein, bis Helmut Schmidt hier ein Wochenendhaus bezog, Ehefrau Loki Gäste mit selbstgebackenem Butterkuchen und Kaffee bewirtete und der Bundeskanzler von hier aus auf seiner »Mistral« in See stach. Auf die Frage, ob er jemals beim Segeln Angst gehabt hätte, sagt Schmidt: »Einmal bin ich mit der Jolle gekentert. Das ist normal für einen Jollensegler. Er muss in der Lage sein, das Boot allein wieder aufzurichten. Aber das Wasser war scheißkalt, es war um Ostern herum, und ich hatte Angst – nicht vor dem Wasser, sondern vor einem Herzschlag.«

SKIPPER SCHMIDT

Lake Brahmsee used to be an inconspicuous water in Schleswig-Holstein until Helmut Schmidt moved to a weekend house here, with his wife serving homemade butter cake and coffee to their guests and the Chancellor putting to sea from there on board of his »Mistral«. When asked if he had ever been afraid while sailing, Schmidt answered: »My dinghy capsized once. That is normal for a dinghy sailor. He must be able to right the boat alone again. But the water was damn cold, it was around Easter, and I was afraid – however, not of the water, but of a heart failure.«

KLUGE KÖPFE / SMART MINDS **109**

KREUZFAHRER KÖHLER
Sechs Tage hatte der Bundespräsident 2008 in Nigeria verbracht, um dort über den Ausbau einer wichtigen Energiepartnerschaft zwischen dem westafrikanischen Staat und Deutschland zu verhandeln. Bei einer Rundfahrt durch den Hafen von Lagos löste sich bei Horst und Eva Luise Köhler die ganze Anspannung der anstrengenden Reise.

CRUSADER KOEHLER
In 2008, Federal President had spent six days in Nigeria to conduct negotiations on the expansion of a major energy partnership between the West African country and Germany. During a tour through the port of Lagos, all of Horst and Eva Luise Koehler's tension of the strenuous journey got loose.

SCHIFFSMALER
Der Maler Gustav Klimt verbrachte zwischen 1900 und 1916 viele Sommer am Attersee. Ein Großteil seiner berühmten Landschaftsgemälde zeigt die umliegenden Wälder und blühenden Wiesen aus Sicht des Ruderers Klimt.

MARINE ARTIST
Between 1900 and 1916, the painter Gustav Klimt spent many summers at Lake Attersee. Most of his famous landscape paintings show the surrounding forests and flowering meadows from the perspective of the rower Klimt.

WASSERMUSIK
Herbert von Karajan liebte nicht nur die Musik, er begeisterte sich auch für schöne Frauen, Sportwagen, Flugzeuge und Yachten. Mit seiner »Helisara« nahm er an zahlreichen Regatten teil. Und da Karajan ein Maestro war, ging er aus fast allen Rennen als Sieger hervor.

WATER MUSIC
Herbert von Karajan not only loved music, he was also enthusiastic about beautiful women, sports cars, aircraft and yachts. With his »Helisara« he took part in many regattas. Since Karajan was a maestro, he emerged victorious from nearly all races.

SCHWERE LAST
Wenn sich Helmut Kohl und Boris Jelzin zu brisanten Gesprächen trafen, dann mitunter an ungewöhnlichen Orten – zum Beispiel in der Sauna oder 1998 auf dem sibirischen Baikalsee. Das Thema der beiden politischen Schwergewichte hier war der russische Truppenabzug aus Deutschland. Eine Angelpartie trug zwischendurch zur Entspannung bei.

HEAVY WEIGHT
When Helmut Kohl and Boris Yeltsin met for highly sensitive discussions, they sometimes met in unusual places – for example, in the sauna, or as in 1998 on the Siberian Lake Baikal. The topic of the two political heavy weights was the withdrawal of the Russian armed forces from Germany. A fishing trip in between contributed to relaxation.

GROSSE GESTE
In diesem Ruderboot haben schon viele berühmte Menschen gesessen. Der Regierungschef der UdSSR Nikita Chruschtschow zum Beispiel oder Kofi Annan, als er noch Generalsekretär der Vereinten Nationen war. Im Spätsommer 2008 kam diese Ehre nun Angela Merkel zuteil, die von Premierminister Fredrik Reinfeldt über den Harpsundsee vor dem Landsitz der schwedischen Regierung gerudert wurde.

GREAT GESTURE
Many famous people already sat in this rowboat. The head of government of the USSR Nikita Khrushchev, for example, or Kofi Annan, when he was Secretary General of the United Nations. In late summer of 2008, this honour was awarded to Angela Merkel who was rowed by Prime Minister Fredrik Reinfeldt across Lake Harpsund in front of the country estate of the Swedish Government.

DIPLOMATISCHER DIENST
Ernste Themen in lockerer Umgebung anzusprechen, darauf verstand sich Bundeskanzler Willy Brandt Anfang der 1970er-Jahre. Mit dem sowjetischen Staats- und Parteichef Leonid Breschnew rauschte er über das Schwarze Meer. Entspannt ging es auch vor Longboat Key in Florida zu, wo sich Brandt mit Richard Nixon getroffen hatte und sich danach beim Angeln mit Lunchpaket und Bier erholte.

DIPLOMATIC SERVICE
Addressing serious topics in a relaxed environment – something which in the early 1970s Chancellor Willy Brandt was an expert in. With the Soviet head of state and party leader Leonid Brezhnev he rushed across the Black Sea. Also at Longboat Key in Florida it was relaxed, where Brandt had met with Richard Nixon, recovering afterward with fishing, lunch package and beer.

VORM WIND
Mit vollen Segeln voraus, so schätzte es Karl Schiller — als erster deutscher Superminister Anfang der 1970er-Jahre sowie am Ruder mit Ehefrau Etta.

DOWNWIND
On course with full sails, that's how Karl Schiller liked it — as the first German superminister in the early 1970s as well as at the helm together with wife Etta.

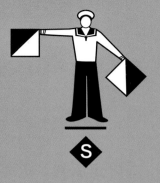

HELMUT SCHMIDT
FÜNFTER BUNDESKANZLER DER BUNDESREPUBLIK DEUTSCHLAND
FIFTH CHANCELLOR OF THE FEDERAL REPUBLIC OF GERMANY

»ICH SCHÄTZE DIE OFFENE ELBE, DIE NORDSEE UND DIE OSTSEE. DA IST DIE FREIHEIT DES SEGLERS. ICH BIN SEIT MEINEM VIERZEHNTEN LEBENSJAHR EIN SEGLER.«

»I APPRECIATE THE OPEN ELBE, THE NORTH SEA AND THE BALTIC SEA. THERE THE SAILOR FINDS HIS LIBERTY. I HAVE BEEN A SAILOR SINCE MY 14TH BIRTHDAY.«

FILM AB
SHOWTIME

Ob im Sturm der Gefühle, ob allein oder mit einem Tiger in den unendlichen Weiten des Ozeans, ob im Herzen froh, aber dem Untergang geweiht – ein Boot ist immer eine sichere Bühne für einen guten Film.

Be it in the rush of feelings, be it alone or with a tiger in the vastness of the ocean, whether glad at heart, but doomed – a boat is always a safe stage for a good movie.

RÄTSELHAFTE EREIGNISSE
Der irre Graf Olaf (Jim Carey) blickt im Film »Lemony Snicket – Rätselhafte Ereignisse« mit den Kindern Violet, Klaus und Sunny in das Auge eines nahenden Orkans.

UNFORTUNATE EVENTS
In the movie »Lemony Snicket – A Series Of Unfortunate Events« the crazy Count Olaf (Jim Carey) and the children Violet, Klaus and Sunny looking into the eye of a hurricane.

FILM AB / SHOWTIME **121**

LIFE OF PI – SCHIFFBRUCH MIT TIGER
Allein mit einer hungrigen Bestie in einem Boot, das erleben Schiffsreisende eher selten. Der Film spielte 609 Millionen Dollar ein.

LIFE OF PI – SHIPWRECKED WITH A TIGER
To be alone with a hungry beast on a boat, an experience ship passengers will rather rarely make. The movie brought in 609 million Dollars.

◀ **DER STURM & ALL IS LOST**
Fischer Billy (George Clooney; oben) will sich mit dem Sturm messen – und riskiert dabei Kutter und Crew. Robert Redford hingegen kämpft allein um sein Leben.

THE STORM & ALL IS LOST
Fisherman Billy (George Clooney; above) wants to match the storm – risking cutter and crew. Robert Redford, on the other hand, fights for his life alone.

DER KNABE AUF DEM DELPHIN
Sophia Loren 1957 als Schwammtaucherin Phaedra in typischer Arbeitskleidung – so wie Poseidon sie schuf.

THE BOY ON A DOLPHIN
Sophia Loren in 1957 as sponge diver Phaedra in typical workwear – as Poseidon created her.

KÖNIGIN CHRISTINE
Die junge Königin (Greta Garbo) verzichtet für die Liebe auf den schwedischen Thron und reist per Schiff nach Spanien in eine ungewisse Zukunft.

QUEEN CHRISTINE
The young queen (Greta Garbo) abdicates the throne for love and travels to Spain by ship to face an uncertain future.

TITANIC
Dem Untergang geweiht, aber in Liebe vereint – nie war eine Schiffstragödie schmalziger inszeniert als hier: »Titanic« von James Cameron, in den Hauptrollen mit Leonardo Di Caprio und Kate Winslet, heimste 1998 elf Oscars ein.

TITANIC
Doomed but united in love – never has a sea tragedy been staged more sentimental than here: »Titanic« by James Cameron, featuring Leonardo Di Caprio and Kate Winslet, was awarded with eleven Oscars in 1998.

◀ DIE OBEREN ZEHNTAUSEND
Grace Kelly gibt die verwöhnte Daisy, Bing Crosby ihren Ex-Mann – gemeinsam singen sie hier »True Love«. Die Hollywoodinszenierung nimmt das spätere Society-Leben von Grace Kelly vorweg. Zugleich ist es ihr letzter Film, bevor sie 1956 Fürst Rainier III. von Monaco heiratet.

HIGH SOCIETY
Grace Kelly performing the spoiled Daisy, Bing Crosby plays her husband – here, they sing »True Love« together. The Hollywood production anticipates Grace Kelly's future society life. At the same time, it is her last movie before marrying Prince Rainier III of Monaco in 1956.

HEREIN, OHNE ANZUKLOPFEN
Wie viele Seemänner, hat auch Bill (Richard Todd) in jedem Hafen eine Braut. So kommt es, wie es kommen muss: Alle wollen ein Stück von ihm. Die englische Filmkomödie kam 1962 in die Kinos.

DON'T BOTHER TO KNOCK
Like many sailors, also Bill (Richard Todd) has a chick in each port. And thus, as it must happen: Everyone wants a piece of him. In 1962 the English comedy movie was shown in the cinemas.

FLUCH DER KARIBIK
Der beste Piratenfilm seit Errol Flynn nicht mehr segelt: Der exzentrische Captain Jack Sparrow (Johnny Depp) hilft, die schöne Tochter des Gouverneurs aus den Klauen des ruchlosen Piraten Barbossa zu befreien und gerät dabei von einem verrückten Abenteuer in das nächste.

PIRATES OF THE CARIBBEAN
The best pirate movie since Errol Flynn no longer sails: The eccentric captain Jack Sparrow (Johnny Depp) helps freeing the beautiful daughter of the governor from the clutches of the nefarious pirate Barbossa and incurs one crazy adventure after the other.

LEGENDEN DER LEIDENSCHAFT
In dem US-Heimatfilm von 1994 spielt Brad Pitt den kernigen Sohn eines Ranchers, der im Streit um eine Frau zum Mörder wird. Auf der Flucht schlägt er sich zu Lande und zu Wasser durch – als Pferdedieb und Schmuggler.

LEGENDS OF THE FALL
In the US movie from 1994 with regional background, Brad Pitt plays the pithy son of a rancher who becomes a murderer in a fight over a woman. While on the run he muddles through on land as well as on water – as a horse thief and smuggler.

MANCHE MÖGEN'S HEISS
Eine Yacht als absolute Verheißung von Glück und Liebe – davon träumt Ukulelespielerin Sugar (Marilyn Monroe) in der US-Filmkomödie von 1959. Am Strand verliebt sie sich in den vermeintlichen Shell-Erben Joe (Tony Curtis). Dass der ihr in Wahrheit etwas vorgaukelt, erkennt sie nicht. Denn Sugar sieht nur die Yacht und das damit verbundene Leben ohne Sorgen.

SOME LIKE IT HOT
A yacht as an absolute promise of happiness and love – this is what ukulele player Sugar (Marilyn Monroe) is dreaming about in the US comedy film of 1959. On the beach she falls in love with the alleged Shell heir Joe (Tony Curtis). She does not realize that he is deceiving her. Sugar has only eyes for the yacht and the associated life without worries.

FILM AB / SHOWTIME **132**

KAMERA AB & LEINEN LOS

(1) Joan Collins erholt sich von anstrengenden Dreharbeiten zum Historienschinken »Die jungfräuliche Königin«. (2) Raquel Torres und Josephine Dunn üben sich im Balanceakt auf einem Wasserflugzeug. (3) »Die barfüßige Gräfin« Ava Gardner macht sich lang. (4) Nicht die Monroe, aber ihre Pose – Bibi Johns frohlockt im »Hafen unserer Träume«. (5) Virgina Grey sucht am Horizont nach ihrem Liebsten. (6) Giovanna Ralli bangt auf einem schnellen Boot um ihr Kopftuch. (7) Gary Cooper gibt sich auch im Urlaub an Bord, wie ihn das Publikum liebte – als schweigsamer Held. (8) Stummfilmstar Clara Bow zeigt sich bei einer Homestory auf ihrem Boot flexibel. (9) Mode- und Stilikone Audrey Hepburn bezaubert als »Sabrina«. (10) Ein ganzes Schiff voller Piratinnen wartet darauf, in Long Beach fette Männerbeute zu machen.

ACTION & CAST OFF

(1) Joan Collins recovering from the strenuous shooting for the historic blockbuster »The maiden queen«. (2) Raquel Torres and Josephine Dunn practising the balancing act on a waterplane. (3) »The Barefoot Contessa« Ava Gardner stretching out. (4) Not the Monroe, but her pose – Bibi Johns rejoicing in »Hafen unserer Träume«. (5) Virginia Grey searching the horizon for her darling. (6) Giovanna Ralli is worried about her headscarf on a fast boat. (7) Also on holiday Gary Cooper acting like the audience loves him – as a silent hero. (8) During a home story, silent movie star Clara Bow proves to be flexible on her boat. (9) Fashion and style icon Audrey Hepburn being charming as »Sabrina«. (10) An entire ship full of female pirates waiting to make male prey.

FILM AB / SHOWTIME 134

KINOWERBUNG
Hollywood-Traumpaar Tony Curtis und Janet Leigh auf einem Werbefoto von 1955.

CINEMA ADVERTISING
Hollywood dream couple Tony Curtis and Janet Leigh on a promotional photo of 1955.

BUSTER KEATON STORY ▶
Das Schiff ist noch an Land, doch der Kapitän (Donald O'Connor) sticht schon in See. Filmszene von 1957.

BUSTER KEATON STORY
The ship is still ashore but the captain (Donald O'Connor) is already putting to sea. Movie scene from 1957.

TANZEINLAGE
Schauspielerin Abbe Lane war bekannt dafür, dass sie plötzlich zu tanzen begann, wenn sie sich besonders freute. Hier legt sie bei den Filmfestpielen von Venedig 1956 ein Tänzchen auf dem Dach eines Wassertaxis hin. Einlagen wie diese brachten ihr daher in den USA den Titel »Schwungvollste Sexbombe im Show-Geschäft« ein.

DANCE NUMBER
Actress Abbe Lane was known to suddenly start dancing when she was particularly pleased. Here she dances on the roof of a water taxi during the Venice film festival in 1956. Interludes like this made her earn the title »Liveliest sexbomb in the showbiz« in the US.

VIER ENGEL FÜR VICTORIA
Ein Vertrag als Engel zählt zu den lukrativsten Jobs, die ein Model haben kann. Das Unterwäsche-Label Victoria's Secret entlohnt die Arbeit seiner Engel mit einem siebenstelligen Betrag. Als Arbeit gilt auch dieses Fotoshooting auf einer Yacht in Florida.

FOUR ANGELS FOR VICTORIA
A contract as angel is one of the most lucrative jobs a model can have. The lingerie label Victoria's Secret remunerates the work of its angels with a seven-digit sum. Also this photo shooting on a yacht in Florida is considered to be work.

AM WILDEN FLUSS
Eigentlich wollte Gail (Meryl Streep) mit Mann und Kindern nur eine Bootsfahrt auf einem Wildbach machen. Doch als zwei flüchtige Bankräuber zusteigen, wird aus dem Familienausflug ein Horrortrip.

THE RIVER WILD
Gail (Mery Streep) actually wanted to enjoy a boat trip on a torrent with her husband and children. However, when two fugitive bank robbers climb on board, the family outing becomes a horror trip.

LEBEN UND STERBEN LASSEN
Die Zutaten für einen erfolgreichen James-Bond-Film sind einfach: Ein Bösewicht, schöne Frauen, schnelle Autos — und Boote. So wie hier 1973 mit Roger Moore.

LIVE AND LET DIE
The ingredients of a successful James Bond movie are simple: A bad guy, beautiful women, fast cars — and boats. Just like here in 1973 with Roger Moore.

DIE WELT IST NICHT GENUG
James Bond (Pierce Brosnan) verfolgt 1999 mit diesem turbinengetriebenen Rennboot eine Attentäterin durch London. Erst als sie in einen Heißluftballon verduftet, muss 007 beidrehen.

THE WORLD IS NOT ENOUGH
James Bond (Pierce Brosnan) in 1999 pursuing an assassin through London onboard this turbine-powered racing boat. Only when she disappears in a hot air balloon, 007 must heave to.

COMING OUT
Wie Ursula Andress mit zwei üppigen Muscheln aus dem Meer kommt, gilt als eine der berühmtesten Strandszenen, die je gedreht wurden. Das beige Stück Stoff, das sie dabei trug, ging als »Dr.-No-Bikini« in die Geschichte ein. Eine gute Figur machte in dieser Szene auch Sean Connery als James Bond.

COMING OUT
One of the most famous beach scenes ever shot shows Ursula Andress coming out of the sea with two opulent shells. The beige piece of cloth she was wearing then went down in history as »Dr. No Bikini«. In this scene, also Sean Connery cut a good figure as James Bond.

WINKERALPHABET / SEMAPHORE ALPHABET **143**

Das Winkeralphabet wurde einst zur optischen Kommunikation auf See erfunden. Abhängig davon, wie die zwei quadratischen, in Gelb und Rot geteilten Flaggen gehalten werden, ergeben sich die Buchstaben. Die United States Navy nutzt das Winkeralphabet zum Teil heute noch, da es im Gegensatz zum Funkverkehr als abhörsicher gilt.

The semaphore was once invented for optical communications at sea.
Depending on how two square flags, divided in yellow and red portions, are held, you get different letters. The United States Navy partly use the semaphore even today because in contrast to radio communications it is deemed tap-proof.

WAHRSCHAUER
Werbung für Schwimmwesten aus Kork, ca. 1900.

WAHRSCHAUER
Advertisement for life jackets made of cork, approx. 1900.

Bibliografische Information der Deutschen Nationalbibliothek
Die Deutsche Nationalbibliothek verzeichnet diese Publikation
in der Deutschen Nationalbibliografie; detaillierte bibliografische
Daten sind im Internet über http://dnb.dnb.de abrufbar.

Bibliographic information published by the German National Library
The German National Library lists this publication in the German National
Bibliography; Detailed bibliographic data can be found online at http:dnb.dnb.de

1. Auflage / 1. Edition
ISBN 978-3-7688-3836-8
© Delius, Klasing & Co. KG, Bielefeld

LAYOUT UND REDAKTION / LAYOUT AND EDITORIAL
BEHNKEN & PRINZ GmbH & Co. KG

HERAUSGEBER / EDITORS
Wolfgang Behnken, Leonard Prinz

TEXT
Leonard Prinz

LEKTORAT / EDITOR
Birgit Radebold

ÜBERSETZUNG / TRANSLATION
Vincenzo Ferrara/ade team Stuttgart

LAYOUT
Anna Moritzen

LITHO
digital l data l medien, Bad Oeynhausen

DRUCK UND BINDUNG / PRINTING AND BINDING
Kunst- und Werbedruck, Bad Oeynhausen
Printed in Germany 2014

Alle Rechte vorbehalten! Ohne ausdrückliche Erlaubnis des Verlages darf das Werk weder komplett noch teilweise reproduziert, übertragen oder kopiert werden, wie z. B. manuell oder mithilfe elektronischer und mechanischer Systeme inkl. Fotokopieren, Bandaufzeichnung und Datenspeicherung.

All rights reserved! The work shall not be reproduced, transferred or copied, either in whole or in part, like e. g. manually or by means of electronic or mechanical systems incl. photocopying, tape recordings and data storage, without the explicit permission of the publisher.

VERLAG / PUBLISHER
Delius Klasing Verlag, Siekerwall 21, D-33602 Bielefeld
Tel./ Phone: 0521 / 559-0, Fax: 0521 / 559-115
E-mail: info@delius-klasing.de, www.delius-klasing.de

BILDNACHWEIS
PHOTO CREDITS

action press: Seite 44 oben (action press/REX FEATURES LTD.)

akg-images: Seite 120 oben (akg-images/Album/WARNER BROS. PICTURES), 136 (akg-images/Mondadori Portfolio/Emilio Ronchini)

Corbis: Cover hinten (Sygma/Corbis), Seite 6–7, 10–11, 14, 19, 20, 29 sowie Klappe vorn, 1. v. o. (Bettmann/Corbis), 30 (Stéphane Cardinale/Sygma/Corbis), 38–39 sowie Klappe vorn, 6. v. o. (Louie Psihoyos/Corbis), 40 (Bettmann/Corbis), 42 (Underwood & Underwood/Underwood & Underwood/Corbis), 43, 48 (Bettmann/Corbis), 79 oben rechts (James Andanson/Sygma/Corbis), 87 (Bettmann/Corbis), 88 (Eric Robert/ Sygma/Corbis), 92 (Sergey Konenkov/Sygma/Corbis), 99 (Sygma/Corbis), 100 (Corbis), 104 (Bettmann/Corbis), 111 (James Andanson/Sygma/Corbis), 133 oben links, 133 unten links, 144 (Bettmann/Corbis)

ddp: Seite 4–5 (ddp images/SIPA), 16–17 (ddp images/United Archives), 21 unten (ddp images/SIPA), 24–25 (ddp images/Newscom/Kyodo), 34 oben rechts (ddp images/Camera Press/Ares), 34 unten links (ddp images/SIPA), 34 unten rechts (ddp images/Camera Press/Richard Gillard), 35 oben links (ddp images/Target Press), 35 oben rechts (ddp images/SIPA), 44 unten (ddp images/CelebrityVibe), 83 (ddp images/Olycom), 120 unten (ddp images/Capital Pictures/Capi), 121 (ddp images/Warner Bros), 125 (ddp images), 137 (ddp images/JPI Studios), 139 (ddp images), 140–141 (ddp images)

Getty Images: Seite 8–9 sowie Klappe vorn, 4. v. o. (Stuart Wilson/Getty Images), 15 (RDA/Getty Images), 18 (Gamma-Rapho via Getty Images), 21 oben (Keystone-France/Gamma-Keystone via Getty Images), 23 (Slim Aarons/Getty Images), 35 unten rechts (Mark Cuthbert/UK Press via Getty Images), 49 (Slim Aarons/Getty Images), 50 (Hulton Archive/Getty Images), 51 (AFP/Getty Images), 56–57 (REPORTERS ASSOCIES/Gamma-Rapho via Getty Images), 60 (Michael Ochs Archives/Getty Images), 68 (Pictorial Parade/Getty Images), 72 (David Cairns/Getty Images), 73 (Keystone-France/Gamma-Keystone via Getty Images), 74 (RDA/Getty Images), 76–77 (John Kobal Foundation/Getty Images), 78 unten rechts (Venturelli/WireImage), 79 unten rechts (KMazur/WireImage), 80 (Menager Georges/Paris Match via Getty Images), 81 (Menager Georges/Paris Match via Getty Images), 84 (John Florea/Time & Life Pictures/Getty Images), 97 (Daily Herald Archive/SSPL via Getty Images), 98 (Hulton Archive/Getty Images), 101 sowie Klappe vorn, 5. v. o. (Hy Peskin Archive/Getty Images), 110 (Imagno/Getty Images), 132 oben links (Hulton Archive/Getty Images), 132 oben rechts (General Photographic Agency/Getty Images), 132 unten links (Mondadori via Getty Images), 133 oben rechts (FPG/Getty Images), 133 unten links (Archive Photos/Getty Images), 134 (Silver Screen Collection/Getty Images)

INTERFOTO: Seite 2 (INTERFOTO/Mary Evans/ROBERT & RAYMOND HAKIM COMPANY/PARIS FILM/PARITALIA/TI/Ronald Grant Archive), 12–13 sowie Klappe vorn, 3. v. o. (INTERFOTO/NG Collection), 31 (INTERFOTO/Mary Evans), 53 (INTERFOTO/Miller), 58 (INTERFOTO/Friedrich), 63 (INTERFOTO/Rufini), 64 (INTERFOTO/IFPAD), 65 (INTERFOTO/Friedrich), 70 (INTERFOTO/Mary Evans/Marilyn Lewis Entertainment Ltd./Ronald Grant Archive), 90–91 (INTERFOTO/Alba), 94–95 (INTERFOTO/Miller), 106–107 (INTERFOTO/Reto Zimpel), 118–119 (INTERFOTO/NG Collection), 122 (INTERFOTO/Lu Wortig), 124 (INTERFOTO/Friedrich), 126–127 (INTERFOTO/Miller), 129 (INTERFOTO/NG Collection), 130 (INTERFOTO/Mary Evans/MIRISCH CORPORATION/Ronald Grant Archive), 131 (INTERFOTO/Mary Evans/MIRISCH CORPORATION/Ronald Grant Archive), 132 unten Mitte (INTERFOTO/IMAGNO), 132 unten rechts (INTERFOTO/Science & Society/NmeM/DHA), 133 oben Mitte (INTERFOTO/Friedrich), 135 (INTERFOTO/Friedrich), 138 (INTERFOTO/NG Collection)

J. H. Darchinger/ Friedrich-Ebert-Stiftung: Seite 108

mauritius images: Seite 142 (mauritius images/United Archives)

Photoshot: Seite 47 (Retna/Photoshot)

picture-alliance/ dpa: Seite 32–33 (RoyalPress Nieboer/picture-alliance/dpa), 34 oben links (Pressensbild Ekströmer/picture-alliance/dpa), 35 unten links (Polfoto Lehmann/picture-alliance/dpa), 36, 45, 61 oben + unten (Maxppp Gasp/picture-alliance/dpa), 69 (Abaca Lionel Hahn/picture-alliance/dpa), 71 (LaPresse alessandro masini/picture-alliance/dpa), 78 oben links (Claudio Onorati/picture-alliance/dpa), 78 oben rechts (Maxppp Boutria/picture-alliance/dpa), 78 unten links, 79 oben links (Luc Boutria-Fernandes/picture-alliance/dpa), 79 unten links (Lydie-Lorenvu/picture-alliance/dpa), 96 (picture alliance/Everett Collection), 102 (Mark Wallheiser/picture-alliance/ dpa), 103 (Cj Gunther/picture-alliance/dpa/dpaweb), 105 unten (Nikolsky Alexei/picture-alliance/dpa), 109 (Wolfgang Kumm/picture-alliance/dpa), 112 (Korneyev/picture-alliance/dpa), 113 sowie Klappe vorn, 2. v. o. (Eivind Vogel-Rudin/picture-alliance/dpa), 114 (Horst Ossinger/picture-alliance/dpa), 115 (Alfred Hennig/picture-alliance/dpa), 128

Picture Press: Seite 46 (Picture Press/Camera Press/Nicky Johnston), 54 (Picture Press/Camera Press/David Dyson), 75 (Picture Press/Camera Press/Gavin Smith), 105 oben (Picture Press/Camera Press/Ria Novosti)

SZ Photo: Cover (Rue des Archives/SZ Photo), Seite 22, 26 oben (Rue des Archives/SZ Photo), 52 (Scherl/SZ Photo), 59, 62 (Rue des Archives/SZ Photo), 66–67 (Scherl/SZ Photo), 85 (Rue des Archives/SZ Photo)

ullstein bild: Seite 1 (ullstein bild – Haeckel), 26 unten, 27, 28 (ullstein bild – ullstein bild), 41 (ullstein bild – Philipp Kester), 82 (ullstein bild – Reuters), 86 (ullstein bild – TopFoto), 93 (ullstein bild – Heritage Images/ Ann Ronan Pictures), 116 (ullstein bild – Heidrun Gebhardt), 123 (ullstein bild – ullstein bild)